ANNE-THOLOGY

Paul Edmondson is Head of Research for The Shakespeare Birthplace Trust and a priest in The Church of England.

Aaron Kent is a working-class writer and insomniac from Cornwall. Aaron was awarded the Awen medal in 2020, then subsequently suffered a brain haemorrhage a few months later. Coincidence? Probably.

Chris Laoutaris is Associate Professor at The Shakespeare Institute. His poetry collection, *Bleed and See* (Broken Sleep Books), was shortlisted for the Eric Gregory Poetry Awards. He is the author of *Shakespeare and the Countess* (Penguin; shortlisted for the Tony Lothian Prize) and *Shakespeare's Book: The Intertwined Lives Behind the First Folio* (William Collins).

Katherine Scheil is Professor of English at the University of Minnesota, and author of *Imagining Shakespeare's Wife: The Afterlife of Anne Hathaway* (Cambridge) as well as the entries for Anne and her daughter Judith in the *Oxford Dictionary of National Biography*.

Anne-thology:
Poems Re-Presenting Anne Shakespeare

Edited by *Paul Edmondson, Aaron Kent,*
Chris Laoutaris, and Katherine Scheil

With a foreword from *Dame Janet Suzman*

Broken Sleep Books

ISBN: 978-1-915760-93-7

Cover designed by Aaron Kent, inspired by a portrait painting of Anne Hathaway by Roger Brien Dunn in the Shakespeare Birthplace Trust's collection

Edited by: Paul Edmondson, Aaron Kent, Chris Laoutaris, Katherine Scheil

Typeset by Aaron Kent

Broken Sleep Books Ltd
Rhydwen
Talgarreg
Ceredigion
SA44 4HB

Broken Sleep Books Ltd
Fair View
St Georges Road
Cornwall
PL26 7YH

Contents

FOREWORD
Dame Janet Suzman

On pages 28 and 29 of this lovely book you'll find all you might like to know about Anne's long days bereft of Will. Both capture something magical of the humour and fatalism you wish on her because Anne is guesswork; we know virtually nothing. Surprisingly though, Nothing has produced quite Something; this buried woman has tickled entrancing poetry out of a gorgeous range of people.

Included among the twenty sonnets are six by nine year-olds from Holy Trinity School in Stratford-upon-Avon, all of whom have a sweet, sad insight into the death of a peer, Hamnet.

There are seventy-eight poets represented (sixty-seven of which are newly commissioned) and forty-two are women including Wendy Cope, whose thoughtful sonnet ends 'we cannot wish you'd lived a different life'. Indeed we cannot, as it has inspired so varied a menu that tasting each offering feels as knife-edge-ish as a Master Chef final, with a mere pinch of spice too much or too little to choose between each.

The initial splat of olive oil, the basic ingredient in cooking up Anne's dish, is that damned 'second-best bed' and yet only nine of the poets chose it. The others let their imaginations roam through her living days, leaving the end unreached.

Roger Pringle (devisor of so many brilliant poetry programmes back in the day) finds a comfortable marital friendship had evolved, in common with Dean Rhetoric:

> *'The kind of bed you'd offer up to a friend*
> *In need of a well-earned rest'*

Plus:

> *'And where did it end?*
> *She was left their old bed*
> *By her best friend'*

Yet in his first poem of two, Pringle finds a more unsettling story:

> *The best bed's the one*
> *They shared before she moved to*
> *The room next to him.*

(Obviously he snored).

Sweeping away like dust all the misogynistic versions, Carol Ann Duffy offers the most generous solution in her lovely sonnet:

> *In the other bed, the best, our guests dozed on,*
> *Dribbling their prose. My living laughing love –*
> *I hold him in the casket of my widow's head*
> *As he held me upon that next best bed.*

Just so. I too have always thought that best beds in grand new houses were kept for visitors and the second best is where the loving happened. Will's Will made sure she would keep that bed at New Place when their daughter Susanna became the mistress of the house. I spy an amused glint of a mutual understanding in Anne's eye when the Will is read.

The shortest, sweetest poem is a reminder of that initiating moment in Cat Weatherill's 'On Seeing Forget Me Nots in Henley Street garden, spring 1588':

> *I am here*
> *And I shall remain*
> *Steadfast*
> *Contained*
>
> *But on a day like this*
> *When the rain falls soft on your lashes and lips*
> *Remember, my love, that moment of bliss*
> *When rain fell upon us, down by the brook,*
> *And love felt eternal.*

How I wish I had the space to offer more memorable quotes to show the pleasure I have had in reading these poems, choc-full of every imaginable possibility of loneliness, jealousy, constancy, desolation, in the life of the woman married to a man *'born miraculous – as if a flash of lightning struck the earth just once'* (Jenny Mitchell, p. 75), a man who wrote:

> *'Words by the stone, words*
> *By the hundredweight. Tonnage enough to buy*
> *Ten chimneys, a score of rooms.'* (Lesley Curwen, p. 28).

Those chimneys she swept and those rooms she cleaned and that bed she kept warm and he returned to her to die in it. The whole gamut of who she might have been during those patient years are here, and it is a joy from start to finish.

INTRODUCTION

Paul Edmondson, Aaron Kent, Chris Laoutaris, and Katherine Scheil

ANNE-THOLOGY?

This collection is a celebration of the power of poetry to connect us to the past, and to illuminate the complexities of the present. By bringing together a diverse group of voices to pay tribute to Anne Shakespeare (née Hathaway), we hope to create a multifaceted portrait of this remarkable woman, and to honour her enduring influence. The insights offered by the diverse poets in this anthology can help us to better understand our own lives, and to cultivate a deeper appreciation for the beauty and complexity of the world around us, while simultaneously giving Anne a place in the canon of her own right, a place not dependent on the work or story of her husband but centred upon her.

By celebrating Anne Shakespeare we hope to give her the recognition she deserves, while aiming to highlight the diversity of voices in contemporary poetry, and to show how those voices can be used to explore the richness and complexity of the past. Through the poetry in this anthology we are reminded of the power of language to connect us across time and space, and to bridge the gaps between different cultures and experiences.

Our *Anne-thology* offers a range of perspectives on Anne Shakespeare's life and work, and on the broader themes that her life touches upon, from spirituality and the natural world, to the experience of being a woman in a patriarchal society. By bringing these different perspectives together, we hope to create a multifaceted portrait of a woman whose legacy has been overlooked for far too long.

Above all, this anthology is a celebration of the enduring power of poetry to move and inspire us, and to offer new insights into the world around us. We hope that the diverse voices and perspectives represented here will inspire readers to look anew at Anne Shakespeare, and to find their own connections to her and to the broader themes explored. Ultimately, this anthology is a testament to the importance of lifting up diverse voices and celebrating the contributions of women throughout history, and to the enduring legacy of one remarkable woman who continues to resonate across the centuries.

— *Aaron Kent.*

WHY RE-PRESENT ANNE?

2023 marks the 400th anniversary of *Mr William Shakespeare's Comedies, Histories, & Tragedies*, the first collected edition of Shakespeare's plays, which has come to be known as the First Folio. It is less known that during the creation of this most influential of volumes, while *Othello* was in fact being printed, Anne Shakespeare (née Hathaway) died. This *Anne-thology* seeks to ensure that the quatercentenary of Anne's death will not simply be elided in favour of the sole memorialisation of her more renowned dramatist-husband. We think she deserves a book of her own, and now place her centre-stage, celebrating her memory while engaging with the ways in which her lost agency can be reclaimed. In setting Anne free from the restrictions of being, simply, 'Shakespeare's wife', this collection not only excavates a previously hidden historiography of poetical reimaginings of this enigmatic figure, but brings to the fore a kaleidoscope of new *Annes*, reflecting today's broad variety of female and female-identifying perspectives, social identities, sexualities, ethnic backgrounds, and national or regional affiliations, as well as drawing on the richness of responses from neuro- and physically-diverse creative communities.

This collection mines the unexplored possibilities of Anne's life, presenting some fresh answers to both old and newly-posed questions. Was Anne a writer, poet or story-teller? How did she cope with Hamnet's tragic early death? What kind of relationship did she have with her daughters Susanna and Judith, and how might she have reacted to the prejudices attached to women's social roles? How did she articulate her own gender or sexual identity? Did she navigate her world with a non-normative body or with a neuro-atypical outlook? Could she have struggled with her mental health? How did she engage with, or express her concerns about the natural environment with which she interacted? What might her 'voice' sound like if she were to speak through a different set of ethnic or religious influences to those traditionally accorded to her? Was she a rebel, an activist, a business-woman? What were her deepest secrets? This volume interfaces not only with who Anne was or what she might have meant to past generations, but with what she represents for us today.

This *Anne-thology* resists hierarchies, chronological ordering, thematic classification and other structural principles which might impose overarching social or political agendas. Instead, we have incorporated poems *re-presenting* Anne from different periods, and from authors of varying backgrounds and ages, alphabetically according to surname. This allows for a serendipitous collision of expressions, viewpoints and creative responses, bringing the words of the long-dead into dialogue with the voices of the living as they conjure their own *Annes* from history's scintillating lacunae. But engaging with the now also means looking towards the future; to the possibilities for appropriating and owning the past, and the terms we use to do this, which we are bequeathing to future generations. This is why we were keen to include children's voices too, and we are grateful to Jo Herrero and her staff at Holy Trinity Church School, Stratford-upon-Avon, for contributing six poems by their Year 5 pupils (nine-to-ten-year-olds): Hal Algernon Sandle-Keynes, Tommy Oliver Sam Flynn, Emilia Olivia, Maisie Ireland, Carina Vallera-Satchwell, and Genevieve Anne Marragold Stead. How we interpret history's influential figures, and how we involve our younger members of society in those conversations, matters. Every time we *re-present* the image of Anne Shakespeare, what we are really seeing is ourselves.

— *Chris Laoutaris.*

WHO WAS ANNE SHAKESPEARE?

Anne Shakespeare, born Anne Hathaway (1555/56 - 1623), was from Shottery, a village that lies about one and a half miles from Stratford-upon-Avon. She had nine brothers and sisters, and her father, Richard, was a successful yeoman tenant farmer at Hewlands, a site which has long been known as Anne Hathaway's Cottage. The family was also known as 'Hathaway alias Gardner', perhaps descriptive of their kind of occupation.

She married the eighteen-year-old William Shakespeare in somewhat of a hurry because she was already pregnant by him. The Bishop of Worcester granted them a special license in late November 1582 which required a marriage bond to prove the financial security of the couple, a sort of indemnity insurance. This was pledged by two of the Hathaways' friends, Fulk Sandells and John Richardson, for the enormous sum of £40.

We do not know where the young couple lived when they were first married, perhaps with William's parents in the family's home on Henley Street, Stratford-upon-Avon. Their first child, Susanna, was born in May 1583. A boy and girl twin, Hamnet and Judith, followed in early 1585. William and Anne experienced the heartbreak of Hamnet's death, aged eleven, in August 1596. The following year the family moved into New Place, the largest house in the borough of Stratford-upon-Avon. William was only ever a lodger in London and New Place was his retreat and refuge, especially during times of plague.

While her husband had to spend long stretches of time in London, Anne would remain the constant mistress of New Place for nineteen years. The house had between twenty and thirty rooms, and Anne oversaw all of the day-to-day household management. There was the making of dairy produce – milk, cheese, cream, eggs – and the complicated production of malt, for brewing the family's 'small' or very weak beer. Water was unsafe to drink on its own. New Place had extensive grounds which included two orchards and vines.

Anne was financially capable and trustworthy. In 1601 she was left forty shillings in the will of Thomas Whittington for distribution among the poor of Stratford-upon-Avon. From August 1603 until 1611 the Shakespeares had lodgers living with them at New Place: Thomas Greene and his wife Lettice. Thomas was the clerk of the Stratford Corporation and liked to say he was Shakespeare's 'cousin.' While they lodged at New Place, the Greenes had two children: William (born in 1604) and Anne (born in 1608), which means that the Shakespeares were probably their godparents.

Encouraged by an edict of King James I, it is thought that the Shakespeares planted at least one mulberry tree at New Place from 1609 in order to assist with the nation's production of silk. On occasion they offered civic hospitality, too, for example the visiting preacher who stayed with them over Easter in 1614.

Throughout their marriage, Anne was William's co-earner. Theirs was a successful partnership of opportunity, business, and investment. William died at New Place, aged 52, in 1616 and bequeathed her 'my second-best bed with the furniture', a way of Anne remaining in residence at New Place throughout her widowhood. The house itself was left to their eldest child, Susanna, and her husband, John Hall.

Anne died on 6 August 1623, aged 67, and was buried next to her husband in the chancel of Holy Trinity Church, Stratford-upon-Avon.

— Paul Edmondson.

HOW HAS ANNE BEEN RE-PRESENTED THROUGH THE CENTURIES?

The Latin epitaph on Anne Shakespeare's grave describes her as 'so great a gift,' probably written by her daughters Susanna and Judith, since she is praised as a good mother and caregiver, a woman who should 'rise again and seek the stars.' Although her epitaph has been available in Holy Trinity Church since shortly after her death in 1623, over the last four hundred years Anne has been both praised and denounced, eulogized and ignored, suppressed and enhanced. In fake love letters, novels, plays, poems, and biographies, these various versions of Anne range from a loyal and supportive wife who ran the family brewing business at New Place, to a raging shrew who entrapped her younger husband, from a steadfast and nurturing partner to a 'disastrous mistake' who filled Shakespeare with 'revulsion' and 'sour anger,' in the words of one contemporary biographer.

These diverse, contradictory, and irreconcilable Annes underline the instability of knowledge about Shakespeare's wife, but should also open up possibilities for out-of-the-box imaginings, as this collection of poems demonstrates. Some Annes are devoted wives, others are scorned spouses, but they all serve as reminders of how unstable biographical knowledge about Anne is, and yet at the same time, how crucial Anne is for offering a life story that can resonate with women's issues in various historical moments. Unsurprisingly, women have long found inspiration in Anne's life story. As early as 1860, Mary Cowden Clarke advocated that Shakespeare held women in 'esteem as well as affection' because he gained his appreciation of women 'from the mother of his children.' Anne has recently begun to 'rise again,' to become a central figure in fictional works by women writers, geared to women readers. With imaginative free reign, Anne becomes the real author of the plays by Shakespeare, the hidden inspiration for the literary masterpieces, and the real brains behind the Shakespeare family. In Maggie O'Farrell's novel *Hamnet*, Anne (here named Agnes) is a central figure in this award-winning work, and her famous husband is not even referred to by name.

We can never retrieve the actual historical Anne Shakespeare, a woman who outlived her famous husband by seven years, remains buried between his monument and his grave in Holy Trinity Church, gave birth to his three children, grieved over the death of their young son, celebrated their two daughters, and shared her life with him in some way. While we will never know what the real Anne Shakespeare was like, it is time to let her be the centre of her own story, and to empower the great variety of poets in this collection to create new and inspiring versions of her life.

— Katherine Scheil.

Anne Hathaway's Soliloquy

When Will Shakespeare did chat me up
upon a nimble midsummer's night,
I thought the youth no way backward
in coming forward - this budding Bard
with a word-hoard up his breeches.
There's me thinking that in callow heat
he'd yearned for a night of dalliance
with a woman six years his senior.
A woman, I might add, of some substance.
I could sense he was not flush of finance.
Yet he did say with one of many sighs,
'Tis true there's no time like the now
for conjoining two pairs of eyes!'
To which I promptly replied, 'how sweet!'
And forsooth, it was only a matter of anon
before Will dared to pop the question
(though not exactly on bended knee.)
Should I be saying *I do* to a glover's son?
Yet, I swear our hearts did beat in harmony.
O by ye gods, we'd fallen for each other's spell.
I, Anne Hathaway, am not one to kiss and tell,
but before making our down-the-aisle tracks,
my Will and I (oh, I do blush to confess)
had done played the beast with two backs.
Soon wedded. Sooner still child-blessed.

Enter Your Name

Wondering if in that lifetime too
you were an actress, I enter your name
into a search engine. Anne of the sonnets,
by any other name, it'd be you turned
into darkness— eyes *nothing like the sun*,
but the dying of a fire by which you lost
your *tender heir*, your only son,
the graven child who played
amongst the doleful, inky irises,
those silent mouths you tended—
wives of nameless loam,
speaking the language of their essence,
dying to be born again each May,
perform themselves out of the soil.

Approaches to Anne Hathaway

I.   *Words in "Anne Hathaway"*

hyaena
yahweh
hate
heat
want
awe
eat
nay
tea
why
they
we

II.   *Erasure from* **The Winter's Tale**

                           Is whispering nothing?
Is leaning cheek to cheek? is meeting noses?
Kissing with inside lip? stopping the career
Of laughing with a sigh?—a note infallible
Of breaking honesty—horsing foot on foot?
Skulking in corners? wishing clocks more swift?
Hours, minutes? noon, midnight? and all eyes
Blind with the pin and web but theirs, theirs only,
That would unseen be wicked? is this nothing?
Why, then the world and all that's in't is nothing;
The covering sky is nothing; Bohemia nothing;
My wife is nothing; nor nothing have these nothings,
If this be nothing.

III.   *The Ireland Forgeries*

a love letter,
a better will,
a new play,
—all forgeries,
but one thing was true:
the love of a son
who so adored his father
he went through the lengths of
counterfeiting memorabilia
about Shakespeare's wife.

Maybe this love was like her love, willing
to go to extremes.
Maybe the reason we don't know her,
can't find her, is because her greatest
design was to hide herself.

Sometimes for love, what is real
must become forgery.

a hathaway

lay it to thy heart, and farewell: thou art, and shalt be what thou art in thine ear. unsex me here, from the crown to the toe. stop up the passage and keep my breasts for the dunnest smoke of hell. knife the wound beyond this ignorant present. beguile the time, the time; the serpent under't must be provided for. contend against those of old, and the dignities heap'd up to them. art thou afeard to be the same as thou art in desire? wouldst thou live letting 'i dare not' wait upon 'i would'? what beast was't, then, that made you break? when you durst to be more, be so much more. they have made themselves and in my face. i have pluck'd my nipple from his boneless gums and dash'd the brains out - screw your courage. the warder of receipt, of reason - their natures lie. what cannot you and i perform?

who dares receive their daggers ready, speak now - wash this filthy witness from your hand. 'tis the eye of childhood that fears unbecoming. safer dwell in doubtful nature, not eterne. pray you, pronounce the cheer not often vouch'd with welcome - extend the painting of your fear. a woman's story spoils the pleasure of the most admired. stand not upon the order - out, i say! 'tis time to do't. what need we fear who knows? none can call our power a wife. where is she now? no more o' that, my lord, no more. here's the smell of blood. come, come, give me your hand.

Span

after Richard Siken

'Very little is known about her life beyond a few references in legal documents.'
— *Wikipedia*

A person's word for female swan is *pen*. A swan's word is different, more airy, less plosive. An implement for persons writing words is a pen. A pen's origin is a person's appendage, wet with pigment. A swan's origin is a cygnet and vice versa. A later pen is made from a feather. A person's word for this pen is *quill*. An ideal feather for quills is apparently a female swan's, which are large in the shaft and sturdy, so perfect for a person's big signature. A swan's opinion is different, as an ideal feather to a swan is good for flying. A body with inborn chambers of air is ideal for flying. An ideal person is relative, irrespective of what's been recorded. An ideal person to a swan has seeds in their pocket. Sycamore seeds have wings like swans and launch in pairs like they're flying. An ideal seed is an origin. *The Swan* is a theatre in Stratford-on-Avon, launched, according to records, in May '86. A word for this theatre is *intimate*. The ideal origin of a person is intimate. A word's an inadequate carriage.

God's Favour, Anne

'[M]y turquoise... I would not have given it for a wilderness of monkeys.'
— Shylock, *The Merchant of Venice*

Turquoise, he gave her turquoise, like the queen
whose hand, pale and slender, manages her own --
the quill, the knife, the gist of the matter --

the leaves, the trees, the
bark, and the running sap, wax
sealing promises to courtiers
who wait for her to drop curlicues
of grace, remnants of her petticoat
torn by the latch on the windowpane.

[At what time will they hang her.
At what time will they declare her dead?]

Last night she stole in to see her love
would he, would he have her?

He said he would kiss her underneath
the oak, the white birch, the ash,
her hand splayed upon the bark,
fragments beneath her nails.
She did not wash for days,
the rich scent.

Queen, you say?
Queen, I say, for the one
God has favoured.
Seal her, seal her,
underneath her nails,
there the blood runs.

Three trees standing in a wood.
Gold, frankincense and myrrh,
branches laden with words.
Unto us a child is born,
prayers for the one
God favours.

She stands beneath the window
tall as a cypress tree and her name
was Agnes before it was Anne
while the trees, rich in scent, bend.

[Always in mourning
for her mother, though no one remembers.
Where is Leah? Under the cypress trees
she stands tall and the wind
cannot break her].

She runs as daughters will from their
father, once a bachelor who loved
a woman as she now loves a man
underneath the window bending
her hand –

will he, won't he, who can say?

But they say - the people of the town –
once he picked up his pen
he was never the same again.
Not hers, not now, not ever,
so she spat it out – the blue gem -
oceans of legacies, boundless, unfathomable,
her hopes willed for him, God's favour,
                                        Anne.

poem for anne

dreaming of the sands of ithica
in a stratford-on-avon avon tea shop
with a sonnet on my cup
where all the walls are painted white
i think of anne
preparing a bouquet of roses for the opening night
of *a midsummer night's dream* in her patience folds
the man on who her love folds
the man who will gift her his second best bed
while she lies in the best
*

a beam of light through the willow
susanna and judith swim for lilies
trees overflowing with leaves
when he writes it brings peace
a quiet cottage with a view of white stones
where the truth is i am not sure recovered
transparent eyes on a vase
in a stratford-on-avon avon tea shop
with a sonnet on my cup
where all the walls are painted white

Anne Hathaway's Cottage (1894)

IS this the Cottage, ivy-girt and crowned,
   And this the path down which our Shakespeare ran,
   When, in the April of his love, sweet Anne
Made all his mighty pulses throb and bound;
Where, mid coy buds and winking flowers around,
   She blushed a rarer rose than roses can,
   To greet her Will--even Him, fair Avon's Swan--
Whose name has turned this plot to holy ground!

To these dear walls, once dear to Shakespeare's eyes,
   Time's Vandal hand itself has done no wrong;
   This nestling lattice opened to his song,
When, with the lark, he bade his love arise
In words whose strong enchantment never dies--
   Old as these flowers, and, like them, ever young.

Anne Hathaway (1894)

HIS Eve of Women! She, whose mortal lot
   Was linked to an Immortal's unaware,
   With Love's lost Eden in her blissful air,
Perchance would greet him in this blessed spot.
No shadow of the coming days durst blot,
   The flower-like face, so innocently fair,
   As lip met lip, and lily arms, all bare,
Clung round him in a perfect lover's knot.

Was not this Anne the flame-like daffodil
   Of Shakespeare's March, whose maiden beauty took
   His senses captive? Thus the stripling brook
Mirrors a wild flower nodding by the mill,
   Then grows a river in which proud cities look,
And with a land's load widens seaward still.

Anne   Hiddenaway

O I was a mystery to him.
        I am a mystery to you now. I've always been   a mystery to myself.
History has written me silent. Has tried to shape a great romance
        around my name. I saw how people took this course of love—
        their weeping, loathing, jealousy. The lies and loss I did not
want.
What more was a woman for? To be chattel, to bear a child,
        to be or not be   forgotten, depending on our fate?   He wanted
        me,
for a while at least. I was never sure   about saying *no,*   about
wrong or right, about   anything.   I doubt he would have
stayed
            but for the heaviness of my shame...

Affianced. Hasty wed. His Anne.   My Will, so young,   so
        clever, so quick with quip and quill...   At least he wanted the
        words
I made in the world of my mind's eye—   he gathered what fell
from my curious tongue   like a hen, pecking up
        grains...

He put them into his plays. Pinned them into Ophelia's, Cordelia's,
        Portia's own throats.   I sense the bones of my voice buried there.
They speak me an eternity still. I am Anne,   immortal.
        London, Anne. Think on it!   Ambition seeks more than heart or
            hearth—
        I smelled of home.   He smelled of dreams and ink.

We talked as the candle threw light across the walls, dwindled,
wept its wax... *Be true to thine own self,*   I said   *and I'll be true to
mine...* London?   Too foul. Too crushed,
too loud, too   many fears. I'm not so fond of alteration.
I need my usual things—   the costrels and chests worn smooth,

the cradle of oak filled with our tiny flesh—

      the suckling, the comforting...   I was too easy

to leave behind.   I remember   his hands, like millstones on

the meal of my skin.   *Parting is both sweet and sorrow*, I said...

I think of us   as if we are stars, fixed in heaven.

From where I am   rooted   to Earth, they seem plentiful

  and close enough.   They are the friends I invent,

           the friends I have no need to reach.

     He created   *lonely*   just for me, I think.

Both sun and rain are sweet. I have never seen the sea, so cannot name

its salt   or   deep.   What is love?   Is it smoke or sighs

or somewhere else,   between?   Something inside me feels broken.

Something inside me is mended by the sky.   You'll never learn

how I pressed my feet into grass,   how I tilted my head to the songs

of birds,   how I danced in swaying fields of golden harvest wheat.

Time has settled its sediment above. Time is only shadows and dust.

I remain   unknown.   Unknowable,

          like a hornbook with nothing scratched upon...

The Marriage

Married at eighteen to a pregnant bride
Eight years your senior, did you think that you
Had spoiled your life before you'd even tried
To make your way and show what you could do?
Perhaps you loved each other and were glad
To tie the knot. Perhaps, each time you left
Your Anne, your little daughters and the lad
To set out on the road, you were bereft.
Perhaps you were relieved to get away.
Perhaps she was relieved to see you go.
Did you miss each other every day
And long for the return? We cannot know
    The cost to you, your family, your wife.
    We cannot wish you'd lived a different life.

Poems befitting a wife left at home

Something akin to the tight whorl of a baby's ear;
a station ill-suited to the neatness of the quatrain.
No couplets: a form that takes a scissor blade
to a neatly hemmed seam, that might act out a play
against a world where the scenery can be dismantled in a day,
reject all beginnings that need an introduction, every happy
ending. Form instead something akin to that tight whorl,
to the wayward growth of a kitchen plot; a form for chore
and nag and prune and the day's gradual lengthening;
for each act of tucking in; for the yearly harvest of plums;
for the way the children must christen the chickens. No elegies -
but instead shape the days and months and years after grief.
See, there is nothing for it. Only a life, closer in depth and energy
to a widening loop of prose.

The bee-keeper

Your words pricked my core, their barbs
sank to muscle. I was thorned, aching
at heart, counting each sentence
you uttered a blessed sting.

Later, I saw you deploy those darts
for guineas and fame. Words by the stone, words
by the hundredweight. Tonnage enough to buy
ten chimneys, a score of rooms.

As I scold builders, rub wax into wood
I hear them drone like a haze of bees
all hover and zoom, abuzz with the promise
of tongue-warm honey and clotted pain.

I know how you use them. The owners
of kirtle and nether-hose whose lips
bloom red with your bane. I have seen
your tricks from behind the drapes.

You have not discerned that I long
to ape you. To stray, to gaze
too long at the ostler's touslehaired lad,
the dairy girl's buttersoft arms.

I, who see wrinkles in a silver plate
the bulk of three births, sweat-ooze
on my face, whose role is penned by you.
I can never stray. I do not have the words.

Sepia token

Me, a hyper parameter of time
service? I saw sympathetic magic
flow from a devilish feather.

The swagger man of temperance,
his travails up the city road, surfing
the emotional tides of others.

Hometown boy closes the show,
but the hometown girl makes sure
the stage is lit. Blank page me –

did I get a look in from my lookout,
lockout, my Shottery signal box,
with second-best front doors, beds

stacked up by a wall? Yes I did.
A silent partner has power, when
couched in the language of withdrawing,

withholding, withouting. Invisible roses
count, even if the only trace of them is
a sepia token, a breath of a memory –

o heritage o mores! Most printed legends
linger, fade and that's ok. To be remembered
forever is luck, to try for that a curse.

All his truths and yet he never shared
the most important: that love is the box of
chicken nuggets at the end of the evening

in the pub you shouldn't have had.
Happiness is always fleeting. And
disappearing. Except I never did. Hello.

Anne Hathaway sits in a coffee shop in Warwickshire, 2023

Windows are bigger these days, but no one
looks through them. This harsh light
leaves dirty plates, cups, spoons, forks
wilting on every table. Napkins that you
could write a sonnet on, soaked with spilt milk.

The girl who served me had the same eyes
as Judith. I was going to tell her, but
she didn't even glance at me, no smile
as she pushed my tea across a cold space
the paper cup struggling to hold its shape.

I want to tell William children are still
dying of scarlet fever, typhoid. An image
of Hamnet rises above the smell of coffee –
I feel that fear again, frailty of a child's last
breath, the suddenness of his little death.

I sip my drink. Just a sixty-something woman
sitting on her own, and no one knows what
I looked like anyway. Students hunched over
their laptops frowning at essays could never
guess my body was the paper Shakespeare

composed his first words on, when he was
a beautiful boy brim-full of dreaming rage;
that I was the ink that wrote his children,
told the stories of their perfect fingers and toes,
washed their mewling faces when he was away.

The tiny jug has grey bloodless veins,
its chipped lip trembles as I pour, both of us
tired of being emptied, routines that wear
like too-hot water. A mother shushes her baby
out of its pram, the queue shuffles along so slowly.

I'm thirsty, thinking how after all this time
I want my husband back, before any of our love
was separated, acted out. Before the world struck.
I want to reach over the table, sticky as honey,
to kiss his mouth. To make all these ghosts vanish.

You Write a Window

This is how you labour through the night
at the kitchen table, tallying up again,
again, to get the merciless numbers right.
You weigh the loss against the gain,

the plumbing or the heating, the buzzing thing
that has to be plugged in to work, switched on
to keep the household running. You are writing
your life in figures. He is gone

and you are awake in the sonnet of a window,
the chiming of a house where children come
and stay. The paper blazes white. The shadow
at your shoulder knows your will. This room,

this page is the sum of all you have to say
and all you have to give, you give away.

A Love Dittie (1796)

Addressed to the idol of mine heart, and the delight of mine eyes, the fairest
among the most fair, Anne Hathaway.

Would ye be taught, ye feathered throng,
With love's sweet notes to grace your song,
To pierce the heart in thrilling lay,
Listen to my Anne Hathaway:

She hath a way to sing so clear,
Phoebus might wandering stop to hear.
To melt the sad, make blithe the gay,
And nature charm Anne hath a way;
           She hath a way,
           Anne Hathaway;
To breathe delight Anne hath a way.

When envy's breath and rancour's tooth
Do soil and bite fair worth and truth,
And merit to distress betray,
To soothe the heart Anne hath a way.

She hath a way to chase despair,
To heal all grief, to cure all care,
Turn foulest night to fairest day;
Thou know'st, fond heart, Anne hath a way;
           She hath a way,
           Anne Hathaway;
To make grief bliss, Anne hath a way.

Talk not of gems, the orient list,
The diamond, topaz, amethyst,
The emerald mild, the ruby gay;
Talk of my gem, Anne Hathaway!

She hath a way, with her bright eye,
Their various lustres to defy,
The jewel she, and the foil they,
So sweet to look Anne hath a way;
          She hath a way,
          Anne Hathaway;
To shame bright gems, Anne hath a way.

But to my fancy were it given
To rate her charms, I'd call them heaven;
For though a mortal made of clay,
Angels must love Anne Hathaway;

She hath a way so to control,
To rapture the imprisoned soul,
And sweetest heaven on earth display,
That to be heaven Anne hath a way;
          She hath a way,
          Anne Hathaway;
To be heaven's self Anne hath a way.

'Item I gyve unto my wief my second best bed...'
(from Shakespeare's will)

The bed we loved in was a spinning world
of forests, castles, torchlight, cliff-tops, seas
where he would dive for pearls. My lover's words
were shooting stars which fell to earth as kisses
on these lips; my body now a softer rhyme
to his, now echo, assonance; his touch
a verb dancing in the centre of a noun.
Some nights I dreamed he'd written me, the bed
a page beneath his writer's hands. Romance
and drama played by touch, by scent, by taste.
In the other bed, the best, our guests dozed on,
dribbling their prose. My living laughing love –
I hold him in the casket of my widow's head
as he held me upon that next best bed.

Gardner

Hear my soil speak; its out-of-thyme tongues
and sage talk, its worm-parsing, its form
and un-form. Tend my sorrel, growing
where the dead reassemble. Beyond the wall,
sheep feed on the common waste;
skirret ends, peelings. All the trimmings,
yet the magpies stay only for tics and wool flies.
Tomorrow, I'll clear the cote with heavy tools,
stir the animal stink with the earth
to save for the second plough. Out here,
I can teach you things complicated and anonymous.
Like the weather, tricking itself into winter.
Like the leaves only good for poison.
Like this needled herb, its flowers attempting blue.

In the poem

I am a soaring Kingfisher.
Find me in the highlands,
air-goddess, blue wings.
Blink and you'll miss me,
fire-flash of neon.

I am the thriving forest.
My trees clamour
in the race for sunlight.
Hunters barefoot on my earth
i n h a l e,
bow and arrow for the heart.

I am the river that turns the town.
Drink from me, bathe in me
to cool from summer heat.
At night I catch the stumbling men
that fall to their knees, slurring
about a cruel twist of fate.

In the poem
I am no mother, wife, lover.
No woman anchored
by the weight
of her own body.

Towards Shottery

My Anne, I'll walk to Shottery,
my heart will write along the way
our couplet for eternity;

my nightingale, my spicèd sea,
your rhyme, your rhythm fills my day;
my Anne, I'll walk to Shottery;

the moon will draw my poetry –
O race of heaven, sing and stay –
our couplet for eternity;

we'll rest beneath your apple tree,
my heart, my crown, my script, my May;
my Anne, I'll walk to Shottery;

that kiss – our bliss – brave ecstasy,
truth tumbled on us as we lay,
our couplet for eternity;

I dream your scent, your mystery:
'I am her Will; she hath her way' –
my Anne, I'll walk to Shottery,
our couplet for eternity.

Anne and the Sonnets

Suddenly one day
Long after he had gone she
Went to the cupboard,

Unlocked it and took
Out the poems, which he'd said
Were all about her,

And never to be
Published. She gave them to her
Brother to publish.

That, she thought, would pay
A lover of whores and lords
For treating her so.

She never did see
That love is stranger than she
Could have understood.

Will Hathaway

Anne Hathaway.
An *Hath-a-way*:
A resourceful one.

Another, like him,
Defined by doing
More than being.

She hath a way,
She finds a way,
She steals away,

Gone.

On the verb's side,
Not the noun's side,
What's done is done.

A player and a player
Play, and make a play,
And further players,

Each of whom,
Will and all,
Return to dust.

But

Will Hathaway had found a way
To find themselves
In other others,

Characters in which, of course,
Not only he, but also she,
Live on.

A Sonnet for Hamnet

Oh William it's been a long day Hamnet is dead,
Our dear old Hamnet has had his death.
There were so many things I could've said,
I would've liked to hear his last breath.

He went out of the house to play,
He was at my own mum and dad's house and was just leaving.
He came home and was dead the next day,
His death has been leaving me grieving.

Oh William the plague is ever so despicable
I feel ever so angry.
Will, I'm ever so miserable,
It's leaving me hungry.

I feel very, very sad,
I feel ever so bad.

Postscript

A hundred and fifty-four – his pride and joy.
So many sonnets from his quill spill free,
obsessed with that dark lady, and this boy
he fancies. Not a single one for me.
"Anne hath a way with her" he used to say
when we were courting. Thought himself a wit.
Stopped laughing when the kids came, went away
to London. Guess who's wiping up the shit?
Structure, he always said, requires a bloke.
A well-built sonnet needs a framework; rhyme,
if stressed, is masculine. Is that a joke?
Does he think I've been sleeping all this time?
So, Will, just to remind you. I'm alive.
Welcome to sonnet a hundred and fifty-five.

The Note.

All very well for you to say
I don't mind mostly, but

  'Dear wife, sorry I was rude
  about the flour in your hair
  made you look like a ghost
  with ample hips from mellow years,
  wearing too many skirts
  does not help plus the irksome
  Time of the Month the havoc curse.
  I return when my play is finished
  and look forward to your tasty stew.
          your husband'

There it lay, a scrawled inky note
in the middle of the kitchen table.

I scrub and scrub with reddened hands
this stubborn spot will not remove,
my apron stained with beetroot juice
a stew prepared from shrivelled roots.
scrub and scrub frustration out, in vain
this waiting game of Turtle Doves.

The coach ride home is long,
Winter's mud ruts delay
or a moll in last night's tavern.
Pox or not.
Will his inky fingers disrobe me tonight?
Trim the wick, sup more ale to sooth
listening in the gloom
stir the spoiling stew
carry on, scrubbing my way through
another domestic performance.

and you shall never want for calfskin gloves

even as you reach for the hands
that made them and find

only blotted parchment
and you shall never need for company

even as his empty chair echoes
the muttering in the market

and if you should choose him for your own

you shall be jointed by mortise and tenon
held in place with three wooden pegs

and he will show his gentleness
in the raising of arms

plain proof of his father's son
paying pride for his Place

and he shall be gone before
the rounding comes to pass

an embroidery of promises
left on your pillow

and they will talk
so let them talk

dear Anne, because

you shall have more than enough
to do with absence

you shall brew beer and smoke bees
press paper and raise women

hold a whole home aloft
with barely time enough to wonder when

or if he is thinking of you, too
enough to fill all the miles from

a gilded house in an upstart town
to a rented room in silver street

and they shall find of your daily turning:
bone buttons, pins and tuning pegs

chapes for lacing and coins for well-wishing
a ring with a lover's knot

tumbled in the church grass

one little peg, come loose
and buried in summer shade

and you shall not escape eternity
for they will insist on speaking of wills

and beds and padded parlour gossip
and they will wonder

if you waited with patient marble disdain
if you lived aside, aslant—

as silent as your un-inked hand
slipped inside a calfskin glove

so let them wonder

of the books you balanced
of the ledgers in your scrawl

and which words, whose tongue, what wit
might really be yours

*Life still goes on**
(April 24ᵗʰ, 1616)

Next day at dawn the sun rose unexpectedly as usual.
The garden chickens clamoured to be fed,
a clanking bucket plummeted the well, disturbing
pigeons in the courtyard where, as usual,
our Judith told the news to William's bees.

Next day at ten the kitchen smelled of yeast as usual
and mourners filled the dining hall. The talk
was all of him, his love of drinking to excess,
his money-making schemes in London, how, as usual
in men who know their death, he'd talked.

Next day at dusk I told them how, as usual
for wealthy men, I'd closed his eyes and washed
his body, dressed him in his cap, in linen shirt
and winding sheet. I said his shroud, as usual
and right, was stuffed with violets, with rue,

       with rosemary,
            for remembrance.

*Speech by Claudius in Hamlet.

Anne (Agnes) Hathaway Shakespeare

anne of hath- a -way[1],
hailed agnes[2] by thy father

rest thy grave recessed those hallowed holy halls,
trinity church, stratford-upon-avon,
alongside thy revered husband the penman,
the bard, the actor, the playwright
the man, william of shakespeare,
thought some, to have done you a wrong
the bequest in thy name the shame
his bed of second-best,[3]
an e tu brute's dagger's thrust thy chest

others, a thought, a trust shakespeare's
long, lingering, lust thy lip's taste,
ever the tasteable and hips, a keepsake
his hands failed not to see nor forsake[4]

anne, the object of iambic tetrameters,
anne, the subject of shakespeare's - *and saved my life*,[5] -
lyrical metrical footings inurned a live, archived
in the bard's melodic sonnet, one forty-five

anne of hath- a -way[6], here
amongst my words lyeth you

O mother of milk and life
giveth thou susanna, thou judith,

---

1   From a poem for Agnes thought to be written by Shakespeare but attributed
    to Charles Dibdin. George Frederick Kunz, *Shakespeare & Precious Stones.*

2   Anne's father's will, listed her as 'Agnes'. Kate Emery Pogue, *Shakespeare's Family
    (2008).*

3   The Will of William Shakespeare.

4   Adaption -'Those lips that Love's own hand did make' from Shakespeare's Sonnet 145

5   Said to be - Anne Saved My life - Shakespeare's Sonnet 145.

6   From a poem for Agnes thought to be written by Shakespeare but attributed
    to Charles Dibdin. George Frederick Kunz, *Shakespeare & Precious Stones.*

mother of milk of hamnet whom
shakespeare, begetter of hamnet,
crafted, sired, and named hamlet after

daunted I,
the task asked I,
a passing verse whose
rhythms and rhymes
speaks your time

daunted I, when how great less, I
who bear a pen less the pen
of a shakespeare can giveth thou
deep bellowing breaths within
unsizable whiffs and whispering sighs
of this verse, daunted I

how much prayer I,
this parchment moves, guides
my pen a disinterring slide,
an awakening, a resurrection,
a reincarnation thy body, thy soul, thine image
that hath flown their paths,
their heaven, its hell
beckoning forth you, anew to greet,[7]

cometh hastily I pray thy posey
and beseech prayer be not unavailing,[8]
to breathe forth the sounds of agnes
rising her tomb, half a way heaven, its hell,
scripted in resurrecting verse of rebirth
to unearth therefrom some tale her tales
to grace this poet's page that bears
deep the fear a pen less the pen
her penman, her revered husband,
the william, the bard of shakespeare

7   'anew to greet' from Shakespeare's Sonnet 145.
8   'breathed forth the sounds...' from Shakespeare's Sonnet 145.

Epitaph for Anne Shakespeare, Holy Trinity Church, Stratford-upon-Avon

HEERE LYETH INTERRED THE BODY OF ANNE WIFE OF WILLIAM SHAKESPEARE WHO DEP[AR]TED THIS LIFE THE 6TH DAY OF AUG[UST] 1623 BEING OF THE AGE OF 67 YEARES

Ubera, tu mater, tu lac vitamque dedisti;
      Vae mihi, pro tanto munere saxa dabo
Quam mallem amoveat lapidem, bonus angelus ore
      Exeat, ut Christi corpus, imago tua,
Sed nil vota valent venias cito Christe resurget
      Clausa licet tumulo mater et Astra petet

                    * * *

Mother, you gave me the breast, you gave me milk and life;
      Woe is me, that for so great a gift my return will be but a tomb
Would that the good angel would roll away the stone from its mouth!
      And that your form, like the body of Christ, would come forth!
Yet my prayers are of no avail; come quickly, Christ!
      That my mother, though shut in the tomb, may rise again and seek the stars.

Translation from Val Horsler,
Shakespeare's Church (Third Millennium, 2010)

You, mother, gave me milk and life with your breasts,
      Woe is me, for such great gifts will I give stones?
How I would prefer the good angel remove this seal-stone from the tomb-mouth!
      So that your shade may escape, like Christ's body!
But prayers do not prevail – come soon, Christ! That rising,
      Though locked in the sepulchre, my mother may ascend and pursue the stars.

Translation from Chris Laoutaris,
*Shakespeare's Book: The Intertwined Lives
Behind the First Folio* (William Collins, 2023)

Shottery

O Shottery, dear Shottery!
Sequester'd in the dell,
Far-famed for sweet Anne Hathaway,
I feel I love thee well.
For thou hast hedges like my own,
With little nooks of green.
Where primroses smile out in the spring,
With violets between.

O Shottery, dear Shottery!
I oft have thought of thee,
When reading Shakspere in my youth
Under the hawthorn tree.
Nor did I dream in those joy-days
To see thee with mine eye,
And tread thy ever-hallow'd ground
Under the bluest sky.

O Shottery, dear Shottery!
Thy cottage by the lane,
Where Anne watch'd oft for singing Will
Beside the Gothic pane;
The garden-gate, the courting-seat,
The chimney, bed, and door,
The walls, three hundred years of age,
Are with me evermore.

O Shottery, dear Shottery!
The breeze that pass'd along
Was full of sweetest melody,
And every breath was song.
The children playing in the lane,
The sheep upon the lea,
The very stones, the grass, and earth,
Were beautiful to me.

O Shottery, dear Shottery!
From out the well drank I,
Where Shakspere oft has slaked his thirst
When Anne was standing by,--
The well within the garden-ground
Where hide the wicked fays;
And O what comic tales it told
Of Willie's courting-days!

O Shottery, dear Shottery!
I may forget the mine
Where I did labour in the dark,
Till nearly thirty-nine;
But I can never lose thy face,
'Tis evermore with me;
For thou art like a little child
I've dandled on my knee.

My head wears a mulberry's crown

and my arms are its branches:
they enfold my own dear saplings
plus a cottage industry of mice
that scurry in and out of my hollows
creating nest-eggs of moss.
Deep-planted in loamy Shottery soil,
I manage my large household with ease,
measuring out fair weight of flowers
to all, whether squirrels or honey bees;
keep enough back for my spousal tree
with whom I'm entwined. A natural
purse-keeper, I invest in yearly renewal
of heart-shaped leaves, shuck off
lean months like light snows but sigh
under frost when kith or kin dies.
I am happiest in midsummer's dream
when I dance in my green farthingale
to mummers and lutes, doling out
sweet and juicy fruits as sweetmeats,
staining the mud with my rich, dark blood –
'so great a gift': I live on, like words.

ANNYS / AGNES / HANNAH / ANN

Your name is any of the above. Delete as applicable.
You are all of these women, all of these girls.
As Hannah you shook your pewter rattle, four copper bells
and a wolf's snaggle tooth — swaddled in your mama's love,
you stared up at the silver-webbed eaves with grey eyes,
blinked with cool blue eyes, with acorn-brown eyes,
eyes that crinkled, grew wide, your red hair in waves,
pale hair plaited, tied up damp with rags for curls,
dun as the shy field mouse, dark as his muse.
You were your parents' sweet Agnes, his Anne aflame;
alone by the hearth in sour rage. Only a new flaxen train
would suffice for you, Annys, crowned with a garland
of brightest green, proud and pearling in that bleached
wool dress, which gaped like a drinking well. Skin glazed
from summer's rays, you trudged fields, climbed
rotten country stiles — a penny for your white veil, Hannah.
You were younger then, thighs splintered from the lath,
thistles in your fringe. So cold, the down upon your arms
stood on end. Annys, do you recall? The lover's season
left its remains. A shiver like a ghost of the stinking elder.
He traced your gooseflesh, Agnes, like you were his first;
did you sign the ledger with his quill? Who struck the flint
for the stove? Who clipped the muck from his riding boots
with the letter knife? Clap clap clap on the broken fence
behind the lane. When he shook out his pockets did you
catch the London pebbles as they fell, smelling of money,
laced with stale ale? Ann, you will grow tired. One day soon
the baby will be dead, dear one, and you will wonder
how he can lie still next to you like this, so peaceful,
his face to the wall. You will loosen his ponytail,
resist an urge to yank the cord that binds. Shake it free,
Ann. Snuff out the candle's flame, let him sleep on.
What is your name, your *life*, if not his to deny?

A Sonnet for William Shakespeare.

Oh, William I'm so sad you're dead,
And as you took your last breath,
There are so many things I could have said,
As you lie in your death.

And as you leave,
As I was lying in my bed.
You leave me grieving,
You are going through my head.

I'm ever so sad,
This is a crazy house.
It's driving me mad,
With this tiny mouse.

I'll be your wife,
For all of my life.

Verses to Anne Hathaway (1796)

1

Is there inne heavenne aught more rare
Thanne thou sweete Nymphe of Avon fayre
Is there onne Earthe a Manne more trewe
Thanne Willy Shakspeare is toe you

2

Though fyckle fortune prove unkynde
Stille dothe she leave herre wealthe behynde
She neere the hearte canne forme anew
Norre make thye Willys love unnetrue

3

Though Age withe withered hand doe stryke
The forme moste fayre the face moste bryghte
Stille dothe she leave unnetouchedde ande trewe
Thy Willys love ande freyndshyppe too

4

Though deathe with neverre faylynge blowe
Dothe Manne ande babe alyke brynge lowe
Yette doth he take naughte butte hys due
And strikes notte Willys hearte stille trewe

5

Synce thenne norre forretune deathe norre Age
Canne faythfulle Willys love asswage
Thenne doe I live ande dye forre you
Thy Willye syncere ande moste trewe

The Ruddy Drops That Visit My Sad Heart

Sometimes I think what are all of those people thinking in their heads. But if you asked them they would say it's nothing. It's not. I can identify the very moment I realised and it was a good influence on me. Chapped lips, abandoned ships, the history of the paperclip. Another day at the kaleidoscope factory. It's like… You'd hope, one might hope, for more than competent clerks, inconsistent jouissance, priests disappearing behind the iconostasis. And never coming back? And always coming back. With new formations and designs. Precious little. Precious little thing. The grain is made to germinate and then halted from germinating in hot air. One likes to imagine a lightning bolt and not the natural decline. Oh anything but my thoughts scurrying away a little more eagerly each year, dash a ladle of boiling water amid the mice, the mites. One likes, instead, a blackout drunk and coming round to the final act with something in your mouth and no memory, rap the telescope against the bass drum. Contacts lost in the shagpile carpet. Shagsphere, Shaxespeer. I'd like to be a very thin old man who says, What was I? You kept the books for… You swept the snow-packed fields… You were a writer. A writer? Did people love me? You were… the angriest little bear, interior castles. That's all? That's plenty.

Darling, Let me Die in Peace

I saw you in the street, holding a brown paper bag,
             sticking up a little old red sign that said it was for
the Vulgarity of Language.
You could be on any street corner at any time
in any place in the world. I saw you in the street,
holding a brown paper bag,
             sticking up a little old red sign that said it was for
the Vulgarity of Language.
Your brown paper bag held a bottle of wine, which I heard
             you pour into glasses. I heard you say
Thank God that it is me who has the bottle, not you,
as you drank. I saw you, standing there in the street.
You could be on any street corner in the world,
any time in any place in the world.
I saw you in the street, standing in a street corner,
             holding a brown paper bag, saying to yourself,
It is a vulgarity of language. I shall be the best person to judge that.
Your brown paper bag held a bottle of wine,
 which you poured into glasses.
And you drank. I don't know who you were,
but I knew who you were.

The Secret

They splashed my nerves against the walls
of New Place when they rumoured your darlings
into my fears. I dropped the warmed pot,
felt its stinging bleed as if it came from me.

So I return to my accounts. Rents counted
in my palm are promises you owe me spilled
upon some common stage. I want to run
a reckless reel into the ungathered field, watch

the sun's settled bone crop my malt, pick it
for a destiny of grainsmoke in my vats, brew dross
to coin and gross up all my gains. There is no root
I will leave unknived to feed our babes. But do you care

how I lapwing starlight in your absences, that I open
like a gutted lung alone, creep into fat without
a judging hand? Do you still cradle how untethered
to reason's grammar we both were, how we let go

of memory's nape and fell to cushionless love?
Now you riverbed a canker in my dreams:
the twinkling Queen who roared at your comedy
is rotting inside. Her light blisters. The palace you adore

is a maze of tinsel and gutscrape. Come home.
The graves in Trinity are quiet as our bed.
A stain of you is holy dust. In your silence I know
I am the better poet when my story snags

on a secret

equal to your wombcraft, hugged beyond a name
you called me in a sonnet once, that grew inside me
when we were young, too young to wed, and smeared
a line of us into doom's thundered crack. Come home.

He is almost ours again. Come home and meet him.

Call and Response

a sad tale's best for winter

That voice of mine you stole –
at least I know you listened.

if I prove honey-mouthed
let my tongue blister

After we lost our boy
your silver tongue turned granite.

take your patience to you
and I'll say nothing

It seemed our love expired
with him, silent in the earth.

what's gone and what's past help
should be past grief

All I heard were words in ink,
murmured as you set them down

bequeath to death your numbness
for from him dear life redeems you

and in Paulina's tone I caught
my own, my hard-won lines.

it is required
you do awake your faith

In our paired minds our child
lives on, flesh of our flesh –

pure innocence
persuades when speaking fails

but I can't harmonise alone.
Won't you utter – utter – utter?

The English Huswife

Clean of body, I dress
my outward virtues,
cover them in garments
which will not meet the pot.

I stand ready to prepare,
in wholesome manner,
this kitchen feast.
Ignore the thoughts of touch

as I handle raw meat firmly.
Meat salted and preserved
by my hands.
Proceeding to cook

and use my quick eye.
Stooped under the weight
of expectation. My tongue
must know the perfect taste.

Vegetables from the garden lie ready
for the chop, the water is outraged
on the fire and I am ready
with my ear.

Source: Gervase Markham, *Countrey Contentments,
or, The English Huswife* (London, 1615).

Extracts from a diary

Hamnet dead. Heart is broken but we must not overindulge in grief. 'Tis a luxury to wail and gnash teeth at the Lord's calling. Will back briefly, weeping like the fop he is. 'You're never here,' says I, ''tis a surprise you recall ever having a son!' Some hours after the burial I find the fool passed out in the dining room from too many ales. Rouse him with a vigorous shake and present him with brandy that he may regain his senses. Send him to sleep in the guest bed. Chambermaid accompanies me to my own, for warmth.

Observed that my neighbour, one Millicent Wrecke, appears to be running a house of ill-repute, curtains drawn 'till nearly midday! Make clear my disapproval, fixing my eyes upon her as finally she undraws the curtains in a sheepish manner, not breaking my stare as I take a nip of brandy. Instruct maids not to associate with or acknowledge the lady for the sake of their souls.

Will returns home in the morning unannounced after months of absence. Rudely awakens me from my slumber, finding the chambermaid and I in what must have appeared a most compromising position. We were merely keeping warm. He mutters something about how I have desecrated the marital bed and it must be left to me in his last will and testament. Emphasises the word *will* thrice or more, fancying himself terribly witty.

Will returned this evening having spent the best part of the year indulging himself in the capital. He wreaked of ale. Looked a wreck having doubtless exhausted himself upon whatever degenerate things men of the theatre are wont to do. Babbled about maidenheads and seemed once more to fancy himself very funny. 'It's not the maidens I'm worried about,' says I. 'No, you seem to have the maidens thoroughly under control,' says he, with a leer, grabbing his crotch, a useless appendage given the amount of liquor he's consumed. 'I know not of any laws against such friendship betwixt women, whereas what you're doing . . .' 'Lies!' he calls out. ''Tis written in thine own sonnet! A pack of them!' 'Poetic license, my dear,' says he, and with that staggers to the guest bed. I bid the maid join me in my chambers.

'Tis rumoured Millicent Wrecke has fallen on hard times since her husband was carried off with the pox and has taken to fortune telling as an occupation. Such heathen sorcery! Remind the maids to stay away, I'll not have their virtue tampered with.

Wake at dawn, take a nip of brandy to give me strength for the day ahead. Instruct the spinners and brewers not to engage in any social intercourse with Will, lest the indolent fool distract them from honest labour, ensure the meat is cured, arrange for the payment of debts. Will writes constantly, stopping not even to pray. Such a thing to exist in the shadow of a man whose sole vocation is a lark.

Today, at my wits end, I entered Millicent Wrecke's lodgings, having thoroughly prayed for the Lord's forgiveness, so in need was I of a room away from Will. His dissipated presence seems to fill the house, wish he would go back to his cursed boys in London, better a sinner than an obstruction. Millicent seemingly triumphant I came to her after my previous misgivings. Made clear I would not be a regular visitor, noted a large spec of dirt on the window, doubtless the wages of a lascivious lifestyle. Surveying the cards, she became sombre, as if to deliver terrible news, 'You shall be widowed'. 'When?' says I, excited. 'I know not the date.' My nostrils flare. Anyone could have foreseen Will would die first, given his predilection for sin and glamour. 'I have some good news also,' says Millicent, cheering a little. 'One day, more than a hundred years from now, a young lady actor shall be named after you.' 'Good grief!' says I, gathering my skirts to leave, having heard quite enough. Lady actor? Thank the lord I shall be deceased before I ever see the day. The thought that such an immodest creature should be my namesake makes me quite unwell. Have the maids fetch brandy. Retire to bed to recover from such unwelcome news. Bid them stay with me. The softness of their skin is such a comfort. Would that I could marry a woman. Sometimes the laws of nature are so cruel.

Anne Hathaway Alone at Avon

To put away love in the grave's safe keeping,
Leaving a handful of roses there;
To know that 'tis only death that is heaping
The silence between two hearts that care—
For this indeed may a woman go weeping,
And yet have a joy to wear.

But O for the grave to invade the living—
To see love die in the eyes love wore;
To know, whatever the asking or giving,
The love that tarried will speak no more;
Lost like the snows in the wild sea's sieving
Is the love that goes this door.

Whatever the measure of earth's bereaving,
Whatever the burden of life's arrears,
O the last-wrung drop of the utmost grieving,
The salt leached out of our human tears
Is hers who watches love's careless leaving,
And faces the loveless years.

The Farmer's Daughter

All through summer there are flies and honey, dark moon or stars with oracles. I catch them on my tongue like words, I ask for the shape of them, that I existed before them or afterwards or how my name was written or to be carved to a tree or something beyond vows and death.

He writes it all down while I remember, who made it up first or whether it was already made, whether he was stitching it to a tapestry or unravelling the sea, astronomy, all our flesh.

I wait for the harvest, measure time in broken leaves or the raising of my womb. I collect daffodils, how I learnt to tell apples and caterpillars apart, which would turn into moths or how long the rain would fall.

I know this is all for nothing when the plagues come, how I keep fighting for all that's left, and that sometimes I give up and nobody knows because I wake the next day and the birds sing.

There are names but none are mine. I was the farmer's daughter, Shakespeare's wife, mother to his children. I glimpse the sharpness of the grass, how mist can shatter a morning, that eyes shine brighter in the meadow and witches keep barley between their teeth.

He's working away or spilling ink, I conjure us stories at night, the same ones, over and over again for the children, ghosts, creatures that roam the house, until I can no longer hold on to their origin, the sound of black holes, echoes of sleep, white lily fungus, where reality blooms towards the precipice.

Ox Eye

You bob your head towards the smallest suns
buttons on a rich man's coat
mooning orbs in pearly dotted nets

You keep your ox eyes turned from us
spread your seed like dandelion in a stiff wind

and if wifeliness didn't live up to it's promises -
a strawberry in shadow -
I can still carve this afternoon any way I wish.

Just now roses are the thing pricking
my interest – they keep their petals on
well into discontented winter
Look at them!
I've named their curling yellow heads
after our children.

Daughter

(Anne Hathaway was described by historian Katherine Scheil as a 'wife-shaped void')

When I was a girl-shaped void
They poured in strawberry blancmange
waited for me to set
couldn't resist a little wobble –
Get too close she shakes!

When I was a teenager shaped void
they filled me with cliches
swear words, mood swings, their fingers, blood
Couldn't resist a dig–
She didn't turn out how we wanted

When I was a wife shaped void
I filled myself with child
forgot their expectations, their desires
And considered my own
Telling them -
Leave us alone!

Gisterland

Dear Anne

I promised I'd get back to you once I'd read the book. The book about you. It looks beautiful. The cover is plain, bright buff (if that's possible) with the title *Gisterland* in white. That Curzon drawing that may, or may not, be you.

Imme Dros gives us a crooked smile from under a black peaked cap. She's wearing large black glasses, a chunky silver necklace. She doesn't look like a woman in her mid-eighties. The short, restless sleep from which your mother didn't wake; the grey, chill November day of your wedding. Precise and vivid. As though she was there. She's crept into your skin, Anne.

A male critic on one of the national papers complained about you being the central figure, leaving Will a 'flat character'. He didn't even spell your name correctly! Imme's husband has illustrated many of her children's books. Perhaps, that's why she was drawn to your partnership with Will, the sparring, the shared creativity.

All best, as always

Note: Imme Dros, *Gisterland*, (Uitgeverij Van Oorschot, 2021).

Wake

You never slept but upright, all of you.
Arms slack, throats held high
like little chimneys. And I,
therefore, your cruck, your truss,
sitting through the midnights.

I had thought you would learn
but on your backs you mumbled,
churned, kneaded pinchfuls of me,
and in the end I liked it, to be
structural. Though I never knew
where you got it, until a bad night,
like this one, two hot heads in my lap,
one on my chest, breathing steam.
Leaning against the bottom step,
legs cooling on the flagstones,
I dreamed of snow, came awake
mouth full of pine and river-dark,
and there he was, boots kicked off,
upright like the rest of you
his head half out the window.

Having it for myself now, the lying,
I pray from my yellowed linen
that you may never rest easy,
that you may always keep watch,
that those butter-round hands
and sidelong tongues never still.

what I told him

he came in once with a ditty about
the armfuls of fruit he'd foraged for us
and I told him that he was terrible
at rhyme   the night of his premiere
I said we couldn't go   there were carols
in the park and I wanted us there
as a family   those nights he tossed and turned
wracked with worry after writing me
into some hemmed-up sonnet   I'd try
to reassure him that no one really
read his poems   no one would stop me in the street
I called him lazy   told him that his work
was not the work of men   it was not
a proper job   he had no right to be
so tired   all of this I said for love
he had so much praise   I saw how much
it troubled him   I had to try and save him
from the crowded world   he needed to write
and in order to write he had to believe
that nobody was watching

On Shoulders / In-Perpetuity

It still exists, this need for exhumation.
    Domesticities picked apart; repackaged,

extrapolated across our years and years in
    continuum of silence. Through a curtain

crack twitching, an orphaned moon sets sail
    across tumultuous seas, imagines a lover's

gentle touch. Beyond continents indifferent
    plague touches all, be it trunk of tree,

body of brick or flesh. This circle a rabbit-less
    snare set in the poor harvest of our souls.

Breadless board. Who are we to judge, or know?
    Except by birth, how we go about our daily

lives until the snapped pleat of a wing, the
    treatment of our own split kindling readied

for the fire. Butter is churned. Sadness sleeps
    in the bed holding onto its tiny white petals.

"Milk and Life"

Woman, I would have been your child,
but it was her
who drank first the milk
of your breasts as from a well, as
from the depths
of Avon. What can be done
in an eight-year breadth?—

> controlling of muscles and fine
>   motor skills

> an abstract mind, broken concrete

> compassion and masking of emotions;—smile
>   robbed and scattered

> dressing and grooming alone, clean
>   and cool as a cat

They came quickly, those August
deaths. *Breasts, O mother, milk and life,*
I had hate away to save my life. There were never
two Annes, six hands
fasting—only you, you
an' my prayers lorn, unavailing.[9]

---

9   'Woman, I would have been your child, to drink / the milk from your breasts as
     from a well' are the opening lines of Pablo Neruda's 'Love' (1920–1923). 'Clean …
     as a cat' is a slight reference to Sylvia Plath's line 'clean as a cat's' ('Morning Song',
     1960). 'They came quickly' is a nod to the Latin inscription on Hathaway's grave,
     which is translated to 'Come quickly.' 'Breasts, O mother, milk and life' and 'prayers
     unavailing' is from the same inscription. 'Hate away' refers to Shakespeare's Sonnet
     145. A smile 'robbed' and 'scattered' refers to 'Othello.'

A Wifely Trio

Love, Labour, Loss

Doctors don't record young deaths –
      children lost, moments before breath –

much less disturb my husband
      with the grief. His mind is occupied

making money for this house,
      the place he stays in town. A bolthole

I have never seen, can't echo with
      the unused names – chosen early on

even though it is not safe. When he returns,
      tears fall beside each grave –

stone triptych I must tend with care –
      but he makes no sound. Wailing

in our room – pain flying from my mouth –
      sees him turn away. In bed,

when I am quiet, he reaches out. Again,
      the weeks of hope, dreaming my arms full –

laughter in the place of gloom – ending
      with a loss. I bear alone, body growing numb.

Anne: Invisible Ghost Writer

They say Will is the greatest playwright,
with a Godly gift – born miraculous – as if
a flash of lightning struck the earth just once,
when he admits my pen writes better. Yet,
no words of mine fly from a page, shot down
by him, torn up, or he scrawls on the back
as I dictate a universe he cannot dream – women
centre-stage, speeches made of gold. Flashing
deadly swords, they transform worlds – man-
made – until each heroine is changed by Will –
forced to lie debased when armoured men
don't shield them well enough, whilst I'm
submerged beneath the title Wife – dare not own
a stage, denied my name on every manuscript.

Mrs Shakespeare Reclaims Othello

My husband did not always write the truth,
eager to defame my love, give it little worth;
but even bodies turned to dust long in the grave,
can chaff a sound when they're disturbed –
mine this: Othello was no more or less Will's shadow,
cast in a hero's shape, twisted to a killer's form.

The Moor I loved stood manly in his uniform,
a rare sight in the town; blacker than an Arab it is true.
No taint of a seducer or base ram – faint shadow
placed on him by Will, needing to reclaim his worth,
ashamed to know I would have left, disturbed
my eyes made light of dark, seeing that as grave.

You look confused. Come closer to the grave,
hear the story of my love. It does not take the form
of that foul play burdened with his name. I sound disturbed?
Of course, I am. But now's my chance to tell the truth –
Othello – black enough to scrape – gave my body worth,
until I felt the most support standing in his shadow.

It was not the same with Will, who made a shadow
out of me – the great man's wife placed in his grave.
I would prefer the box filled with my soldier's worth,
slain by a mob the day he put aside his uniform
to live with me in town. Gossips knew the truth –
Will had another love. I was unperturbed.

But gossips would not let me be as free, disturbed
to think a Moor came to my rooms. They shadowed
us in town, may have seen us kiss and touch – true
love is hard to hide. They chased him to his grave,
unprotected by a squad, his body left malformed
out on my steps. A woman spat as if he had no worth.

I screamed – a widow in my heart – cried his worth
so loud, Will left his other life, came home, disturbed
to find blood on our steps. Even more, my form
had changed – shrouded in dark clothes – shadow
of the wife he knew, going to my true love's grave,
called a whore by Will as if he always spoke the truth.

True, he did not throw me out – duty was performed
even to the grave. But I have always been disturbed
to know my man of worth still has a killer's shade.

In the Lanes Between Stratford and Shottery (1880)

THROUGH dreamful meads, that still his spirit keep,
Roamed the boy-poet, when the morn was young,
And listened while the skylark's mirth out-rung,
Though his own heart was warbling strains more deep;
And 'mid half-wakened king-cups, thought of sleep
More sweet than theirs, that waited till he sung,
And bade it flee; then to his eyes there sprung
Such gladsome tears, as waking, she might weep.

Here with his Love he wandered to and fro,
Yet 'mid his utmost passion of desire,
High hopes, deep thoughts, had room to live and grow;
Here, while he mused of old heroic strife,
His blood leapt through his veins, a fount of fire,
And all his nature glowed with boundless life.

Her Way

Anne Hathaway,
She hath a way; Hath Anne Hathaway:

This passing rhyme by our literature teacher
stuck in my head to this day, even as he
drew us to the magic ropes of poetry
and a love-plotting Romeo and Juliet,
our first Shakespeare play.

But what was your way Anne Hathaway?
Did it lie in the language of your eyes,
the longing look of a sudden glance?
The secret weapon of a smile, or how you said
the things you said? Years later, miles removed

From my schoolgirl-self and schoolgirl tears
(shed over a teacher's impassioned reading)
I visited your home in Stratford-Upon-Avon -
the one you shared with Will - Our guide filled
us in on the life of an Elizabethan wife -

All that ale brewing, preserving, pickling,
(and as his plays soared the globe)
entertaining and domestic budgeting.
I pictured you, head bent in the long night,
adding and musing by glow of candlelight.

Still, these chores did not cancel your mystery.
There are things about you I can never know
or name, but since all the world's a stage -
step out of the wings, Anne Hathaway,
into the applause of your own pathway.

Juvenilia

Unhalve her... Wait. Too arch. Too soon.
When halva's weighed... Sweet, but who'd know?
One harvest's weight beneath the moon...
What moon, man? Where? Best let it go.
Not all things have a natural chime
(none have a / noon ever / own heather) –
if God had made the hedgerows rhyme,
I'd be no poet: a wan hatter,
maybe, scoring lines in kidskin,
with no tongue for love or hate or
hah! That's it! I knew it – hiding
in heart's opposite – no matter.
"I hate" from hate away she threw...
Hate's halfway "Hath," kid. That'll do.

Today I speaklight because yesterdays I listened dark

After the night stars your day starts when your dawn breaks
- Yorùbá Queen Mother speaks.

No body.   "No one placed a loving hand on my swollen belly. I felt a
                 warm blot. And that was my lot. It was too late." She speaks.

foolish young girl
turns wise woman today
unfurl red white
exquisite midwife
of lives lived through
lives lived by many lives
are these all lies?

pale ideas swarm
bloated clouds obnubilate
dainty spells unburrow
like earthworms mating in rain
earth breathe unease
million plus one eyes protrude to deliver us from sin
alas a slow row pricking of alabaster skin
I wishe thee ease of all thy paine

we breathe our last breath   dead delirious
different times we meet again
two souls contort
monozygotic twins
conjoined memories expunged
when you feel the payne
of their burning flesh you impressed
smelt like the glow of their bellows
that howled at night in search of shade

will charred deeds revive?
atone the few by the many?
who waits for me to caress magnetic truths

across time I stand in front of?
I stand well
òtító behind me
ó wà l'ẹ́ ẹ̀hìn mi
assurance envelops me
today I speak

today I **remember** today I **honour** today I **speakact** I today without delay
Anne Hathaway

Translation: Yorùbá to English

òtító: Truth
ó wà l'ẹ́ ẹ̀hìn mi: Something exists behind me

The Poem of William Shakespeare's Death

The sad coffin stood there, bored, lonely,
It was shining in the rain like a dime.
Around the coffin the place felt boney,
By the coffin stood a tree that grew lime.

The place was really dusty,
He would happily play.
The coffin looked a little bit rusty,
He would play with his children all day.

He always went to large London,
A white bird always flew over him, a dove,
He always saw a strange dungeon,
He never got mad, he wanted the dove to fly above.

He loved playwriting, it was love,
He wasn't fierce or scary, he was a dove.

'Has a Way' (2023, 97 minutes)
Anne Hathaway (b. 1982) is Anne Hathaway (b. 1556)

the film opens with a brief flashback scene in
which an unnerving CGI child-Anne/Anne
tends the cottage garden. 'Has A Way' jumps

to adult Anne/Anne, in one of mercifully few
scenes featuring cameos from Owen Wilson
as Will: foppish spendthrift, in oversized ruff.

This sets the film's central dilemma in motion:
how to run a household and stay afloat, married
to a thespian gadabout living it up elsewhere?

The film is Anne/Anne's directorial debut
and, perhaps, tries to stuff in too much,
in efforts to shed light on those biographical

gaps. For example, Judith's boozy wedding scene
while incongruous, does show off Anne/Anne's
voice in a new song (and score) by Harry Stiles.

There's a brief flirtation with romcom,
as one of Anne/Anne's dashing veg-punters
suggestively handles a mangelwurzel, while

a scene where Anne/Anne and Will run
lines – *Many a good hanging prevents
a bad marriage*, etc – is a little on the nose.

Likewise, the folk-horror riffs as a backlit Anne/
Anne stirs homegrown herbs in a cauldron-
like pot, may be one ingredient too many.

Anne/Anne really gets to chew the scenery
in Will's will-reading scene, flailing on
what is (presumably) the 'second-best' bed

(suggestively trailed in another prior scene with
mangelwurzel man). Overall, this perplexingly
short film suffers an overabundance of approaches:

far too many cooks. No Oscars, but if you're a fan
of Anne, or Anne, it's worth a look ***

Peeps into New Place

'I applaud the deed,'
says Mrs. S. when contracts
are signed for New Place.

*

Shaking ink, his spear
stabs paper endlessly till
she bawls out 'dinner'.

*

To keep him from work
she has merely to reveal
her fine syllabubs.

*

When she's glanced over
his super-scripts, he'll sometimes
make a few changes.

*

'Damn', he swore, at work
in the orchard, 'mulberries
have spotted my shirt'.

*

She dislikes wash days,
having to scrub his stuff too,
such a rough business.

*

Relief when he leaves,
whoops all round when he opens
the big door again.

*

As the sullen bell
tolls curfew they sometimes think
of Hamnet ... so young.

*

In Spring he fancies
lovers are flitting between
the cross-gartered knots.

*

The best bed's the one
they shared before she moved to
the room next to his.

*

He looks down the well,
a stone O glinting with tears
of clowns and mad kings.

*

She hath ways to mind
him better than any man
in Illyria.

*

'I am sick of you
lurching in soused; your dinner
is in the Avon'.

*

'Ben Jonson turned up,
we talked of old times, the sack
helped to hide my pain'.

*

All the vital things
were seen to - houses, sword, rings.
'Plays?' 'They'll have to wait'.

*

Following his hearse,
she thought she saw in the street
that lady, turned white.

Making of Her Will

She hath a heady way
to shake her lover's spear
when they tumble in the hay.

Over twenty summers later
she hasn't much to say
at breakfast or dinner.

except news of the neighbours,
the kids and the weather
and the cost of his beer;

while he spends all day
scratching away at 'King Lear'
and getting thinner.

And where did it end?
She was left their old bed
by her best friend.

Anne Hathaway finds sonnets written for another woman under the second-best bed and confronts William and his floozy on daytime television!

Sits there, the lyings't knave in Christendom.
So vile a lout! Sir Knob! Bedswerver! Turd!
Man, what a piece of work. Crookback-whoreson!
Three inch fool, you're not worth another word.

And this woman - an easy glove! My Lord!
She goes off and on at pleasure. Old dog!
Goes to bed to work! Baggage! Base wretch! Bawd!
Hollow-bosom whore! Stretch-mouth, rooting hog!
I'd throw myself away were I like she.
What a slug. Blue-eyed hag! Leperous witch!
Foul slut. Ye, fat guts, stand farther from me.
Pox on you! You tread on my patience, bitch!

Where we are there's daggers, I'll have her head,
Then help him to his grave; the ape is dead.

Anne

Ān is also time in Arabic
The *Now* without excess

Time extracted from the rib
Not the man's rib

A gift, or *the present* in time, for those living on the edge
To ponder time in its lack

To hush ghosts, Anne polishes intentions and silverware
lullabying absence

Other Life

I

I would say, with the stranger's conjecture, that before she was a mother, Anne was a refugee. I would also say, this time with absolute certainty, that she went to the same school as my mother. The UN school in Nahr Al-Bared camp, by the sea. To disrupt monotony, and not wanting to be taught by uptight men, they ran away through the only crack, holding hands, and instead of *reading* and *writing* they taught themselves the principles of living: To hope. To hop from place to place on one leg. Skipping. A game. A play.

A poem.

Hopping and hopping till restless.

II

> *Mother in the camp*
> Do you still remember Anne?
> Anne? That was my other life.

She was so much unlike him. She is so much like us.

Anne, I know how this will read, but I cannot pretend that you're what I imagined. She was so unlike him.

The death of the child affected us differently. She is so much like us.

If we had Greek we could teach it to God then we'd teach it to both of our daughters. She was so unlike him.

You are my blindspot, my axis, my parallax. You are the one thing I cannot imagine. I think of the cove of your thighs. She is so much like us.

I'm a man who is mostly outside of himself. She was so unlike him.

I know you so well and you know me as well, as ever a woman knew Shakespeare. Let's not pretend that they'd know who you are, were it not (she is so much like us) for the angel you married. She was so unlike him.

I am the serpent I'm bitten and apple with envy. She is so much like us.

Anne, when I lay down in Southwark and shut my eyes tight I see more than the world. The past and creation; an eagle, another; drain round me till I'm an immaculate soldier. And down in the middle of me I look hard for my alpha, my aye, my Anne Shakespeare.

My blind spot, my axis (who was so unlike him) my sweet parallax and the one thing I cannot imagine. She is so much like us!

(She was like us when she laid next to him and she wondered just what he was dreaming. No one's read Hamlet, no matter how closely you hold him, how loudly we tell him we love him, you haven't read Hamlet. She was unlike him, who is so much like us.)

And maybe if you'd gone to school and you'd eaten the liberty caps in the Forest of Arden; if you were a man, like my men in the theatre, perhaps you'd have written like me. And she was unlike him.

But what are the chances, Anne? What are the chances? Ben Johnson lays bricks and speaks Latin. And Marlowe is dead and immortal and Homer's made up, or a woman and so much like us.

Like us, my familiar, my mother, my step-mother, just like her daughter, my brother and father, there's nothing more fun than a poet in the family. I was unlike him who is so much like us.

Try to imagine the writer, the canker, the millpond, the little-boy-lost, who is so much like us.

You can't. There is nothing and Shakespeare is nothing. Anne Shakespeare is nothing. She was so unlike you, Anne Shakespeare is so much like us.

Anne, I know how this will read and I love you, I'm sorry I left you in Stratford. We are too much like us.

From a Distance

It was the kind of bed you'd offer up to a friend
in need of a well-earned rest. A place for
a lukewarm drink and quiet contemplation,
where the hours of the day were tracked
      by the pendulous creak of a courting chair

from another room. A bed close enough to bask
in the merriment and joy of the household,
but far enough to grow uncertainties
beneath its white sheets that stretched
      like a dull December mist across the Avon.

It was a place beyond the reach of the Trinity Bells,
where you'd press a finger on the bedpost
and register the feintest tremor of a chime.
A celebration? A wake? From a distance
      the world is still a loving and virtuous place.

Alchemical

Her hand, pressed against a piece of paper
tracing words imagined by her husband
elaborate worlds, a new way to voice
humour or the descent into madness.
She thinks of the smut and thumb biting,
knows as she sits with her child's head hot
on her chest that she can break with language,
has felt death — a grief that knots in her
tongue — a clavicle-breadth of eroded
syntax that bloats the stomach, nauseating
and irrevocable. There is no use for semantics
amongst touch and textures, her feet tapping
on small metal pedals that push blooms of
pale pink memory up through tubes, funnelled
out onto that piece of paper, her finger still
tracing, eroding the shapes and symbols,
unlanguaging what had once felt necessary
while the weight of her child in her lap feels
like a growth from her own body, the jut
between what is done that cannot be undone.

Breadcrumbs

you have a way with flour and water, make loaves
in the shape of words, think as loudly as you dare
leave breadcrumbs scattered in spidering trails, draw
the ideas you have in dust because your ideas
are not welcome here. He came to dislike you
and you came to find his words outdated, his rhythm
disjointed, so you welcome the haze, hating away
at his hat and gloves, turning hating into form and line
scrub poems into windows, make outlines in the murk
stomp out broken melodies with broom, follow
landmarks to the woods. Here you crouch, here
you pick wolf's bane, kneading green matter
into bread and butter, outing what's inside your head
at last, you wife-shaped void, with the second best bed

To have and to hold

They repeat it, her maiden name
like the pun holds her value.
She hath a way to grab you,
she says I hate not you.
Has to give away to the poor and
warms his second-best bed.
What a life she married into,

London to Stratford,
Has him in the summertime
Gives away over winter.
He wrote about their dead son as if he
happened on stage.
She doesn't have him. Only has a cottage
that is no cottage, is a
wife but no wife that gives her name away.

Some wish her a witch of ages,
scour for her in pages

A life split in two, she has a way to grab you,
to have and hold.

A White & Open Orbit

There is another ghost story
between the two of us –

a jug of milk, cream of lead
paint. Leaf turned, ink-spidered
in Diocese records sky-oblong. Here,
the bridge was written

into existence. Your father raised foaming
ships as you, Whateley, became the dark
even master of the sonnets turning the rudder,
polishing each verse to scarred bronze.

Mistress of the sea-fret, rains, you are that bridge
between storyteller and mother, three
lovers an explanation for an ordinary life; the accounts,
a bed unleft – supernova heartbreak of a lost son.

Between the two of us there is another
ghost story.

A Sonnet for Hamnet

Hamnet I am sorry about your death
You were the best, amazing little boy
I am sure you did not like your last breath
You were the one thing that brought me joy

I hated seeing you wearing that gown
I am really upset that you couldn't stay
I am sure you felt really breathless and down
I think you must have been miserable all day

Me and your father were so very very sad
I hope you had a good life before you died
I am so sorry you didn't see your dad
At that sad moment I cried and cried

I have never seen you so very very white
I hope you still have that same inside light.

Turning the Wheel

A poet must have his hungers met,
not just meat but pottage and pies, all from scratch.

Three meals a day and each one eats up a large portion of day.
Anne and the Turnspit Cur work constantly.

Little kitchen dog, encaged slave, bred to work the wheel
that turns the spit to spin the meat to roast it perfectly.

Small animal held behind bars, mounted on the wall,
just high enough above the fire so paws don't burn.

Sometimes hot coals are placed in the wheel,
so the jailed animal must prance like a dancer.

Some men suggest dressing the creatures in collars,
to choke them if they stop working.

In limbo above a seething furnace,
the trapped creature runs in circles for hours.

On a Sunday it is let out,
and as hymns ascend to the heavens
the fur keeps the Masters feet warm.

Such noble work, they say,
to tend to the appetites of a poet and playwright.

Anne reminds herself of this, as she rolls the pastry,
carves the meat, sprinkles herbs to cover a bitter taste.

So Great a Gift

'So great a gift.' *Pro tanto munere.* That's what my brass epitaph proclaims.
My grave lay bare for a year before Susanna and Judith finally agreed on that
phrase and paid the sculptor.

August 1624, my bare shrouded body beneath a light layer of dirt was sealed
with stone and brass on the anniversary of my death.

It was quite the disruption to the altar space, so the Vicar said (complained),
but everyone noticed, though not all could read the Latin.

Judith lobbied for English, so that my virtues would be known far and wide to
all who entered the church.

Susanna wanted Latin, preserving our special relationship for only the educated.
In the end, Susanna got her way, as she always did. *Pro tanto munere.*

'Six Latin verses not worth preserving,' declared Edmond Malone nearly two
hundred years later. And so it went.

Oh, if I could rise again I'd have a long list of reparations to collect.
I'd start with the one who described me as a 'jealous scolding shrew wife'
who should be jettisoned to 'the lowest hell of jealousy, rage and humiliation.'
There's a special hell waiting for him.

And the one who laid me bare in the sun as a 'groaning old crone.'

But what to do with the one who proclaimed me a 'disastrous mistake,' a
woman who 'dragged to the altar' young Will, to that same altar where now
we remain together, entwined in our burial shrouds, dust to dust. How to
make amends for his 'disastrous mistake.'

How to put a price on disgust, loathing, repulsion, hatred. Centuries of
contempt and scorn. My muse of fire can imagine brave punishment.

In the end, best to bid farewell and adieu. There's no glory here. I love on
with my wild heart, on my brass plaque, in my death shroud, nestled between
two Wills. I rise again, seeking the stars.

'So great a gift.' *Pro tanto munere.* It's been there all along. Remember me.

Sonnet 145 (1609)

Those lips that Love's own hand did make
Breathed forth the sound that said 'I hate'
To me that languish'd for her sake;
But when she saw my woeful state
Straight in her heart did mercy come,
Chiding that tongue that ever sweet
Was used in giving gentle doom,
And taught it thus anew to greet:
'I hate' she alter'd with an end,
That follow'd it as gentle day
Doth follow night, who like a fiend
From heaven to hell is flown away;
'I hate' from hate away she threw,
And saved my life, saying 'not you.'

Wondering into sorrow

I will always be connected to thee,
But why did'st thou have to die before I could say goodbye?
And wilt thou be connected only to me?
Thou feelest like thou want'st to cry,

But thou must obey,
Why is love so gory and covered in blood?
But thou can'st not stay away,
Thou feelest as if drowned in deep mud?

I wish I could be struck with thy knife,
I hoped you would never leave,
Then thou would'st end thine horrible life,
But thou art stuck in thine endless loop of grief,

Thou must feel'st a deep, red mark,
But I feel left in the dark.

Penned In

I reach for a quill
find it's not there
and my world falls apart.

Try walk to the kitchen
on one gram of strength,
find the drawer empty.

Stagger to the bedroom,
so far away,
find nothing.

Plummet on a chair
where I'd have finished your accounts,
find my eyes refuse to focus.

This day has ended.
I'll leave house jobs stranded.
A mother with 3 young children. Shattered.

A quill is all it took
to find me hanging over the edge,
unlike you, you never did.

Poem To His Wife

after a Twitter rumour

Imagine being less real than your re-incarnated self.
Less celebrated than your celebrity namesake.
Imagine being *an* actor but not *the* actor.
Imagine being Anne Hathaway,
Shakespeare's wife.

OMG! Mind blown!
Let the conspiracy theory begin!
Where Anne hath a Will, Anne Hathaway!
Life is short to love you only once, Shakespeare
Promised to search, to scroll through the Twitterverse

Of the next life for her, but this I promise you: if ever
Fame in name comparable to a Hollywood actor
Or balding director of The Globe stage
Comes our way, you will turn
Scholarly conjecture

To horse whispering:
Yours the whispers, the scholars
The wild horses you always dreamt of
Breaking somewhere out west, and once broken
They will await your quietest gesture without a word.

* 'Where Anne hath a Will...' is borrowed from @AlphaHanna

Anne Shakespeare: Self Portrait as Hades

I was blamed for taking
Will to my darkness.

I can only say
he fell across my heart
like rain and I burned
to feed him
my red fruits.

Now he
lives in London
and I shoulder the dark
beams of the house,
attend the spirits
we have lost—
cradle our dead boy.

Some declare
Will has escaped me.
Evenings I stoke the giant hearth
knowing the glittered
season will return him

& I grow the seeds
that bind us — dip
my quill in pomegranate ink,
call William to his home within,
my ruby note thrumming
below the streets of the great city,
piercing the passing bustle of the world.

Note: In Greek mythology, Hades abducted his future wife, Persephone, to his underground kingdom. After negotiations, Persephone returned to live half the year aboveground, spending the remainder below because she had consumed pomegranate seeds from Hades' garden.

Shakespeare Country

A week of firsts: cuppa, jacket potato, pint (half),
the sight of two men in the street holding hands.
Mum won't leave until certain I have everything
I need. Crockery, cutlery, glassware – all paired.
A chaste single duvet (John Lewis, eiderdown)
for my bed. The Cleopatra basket for my meds
will hold the Freedoms I'll pluck from the Pride
pigeonhole. Before term starts, we tour the best
of Warwickshire: the rotted molars of Kenilworth
Castle; Coventry Cathedral with its hench Saint
Michael; Stratford's breathful gardens. At Anne
Hathaway's Cottage, the guide insists she was
more than just the woman left behind. Will was
my age, a raring eighteen, when they got hitched.

Why did you leave me?

You are always far away flying free,
Having loads of joyful parties and fun,
So please do turn around and look at me,
A kind and caring and beloved mum.

Unlike foolish and isolated you,
So selfish and disrespectful and bad,
Now this is definitely hard but true,
You're not a kind, caring, or loving dad.

I really do hope you are very sad,
Because of your beautiful son's sad death,
And I am so overwhelmed and so mad
As he slowly takes his last, final breath.

Despite all this our love shall never part,
You will always be in my loving heart.

An Act of Contrition

1588, Henley Street

I know there has
been a terrible
mistake done
between us and
there will be
never no pardon

I have no hope
of life or you
and your love no
forgiveness

I can't bear the
shame to see you
there on the floor
in grief is my
undoing

On Seeing Forget Me Nots

Henley Street garden, spring 1588

I am here
And shall remain
Steadfast
Contained

But on a day like this
When the rain falls soft on your lashes and lips
Remember, my love, that moment of bliss
When rain fell upon us, down by the brook,
And love felt eternal

Anne Opens the First Folio

It slips and whispers on my lap
like overstarched small-clothes;
all I can see today
in the weak firelight
washing over the sheets
is the dark insects who crouch
or stand or bow, curl
or prostrate, swell with child,
carry packs on thin shoulders.
Now, so they tell me, children's
children will read from these,
the stitched, stacked folds
where all the insects hide.
Dreaming I feel him
twist in the night, he cries,
he scratches the dark blots
with tails and swollen bellies
that burrow at his skin,
swarm in his scalp. In the morning
he says, Comb my hair,
sluice the sweat, let them
drop in the basin and lie quiet;
wash where my nails dug for them
bloodily. Love me , love my lice;
love what bites, what breeds,
begetting pinhead eggs
among the roots; love the heaving
boil with its skin. Dreaming
I feel the body shift
like dough, from live to dead
to live to woman to man to
fish and hound, my hands
pleading with it to rise,
and as I knead, out come

the twisting blots and then
the tears, the lives under the skin
to touch, shrink from, finger
again, welcome uncertainly; learn
by heart. Here they are, dry,
pinned silent to the sheets
for children's children to unfix, to let
them scurry in, out and over other bodies,
in the bed's dust, to the world's
end, spoiling their sleep too.

20th November 1611

I write on invisible pages
as I sit on my ancient
window chair. Through the
dark clouds of thoughts
I form dendrites
like an old tree
a tornado inside the bark
telling the sun
where the apocalypse will come from.
This oak tree outside
covered in moss
The smell of malt,
the loss of a teen child
Soon, they accumulate,
breathe out fresh roots
through my feet. They're loud
asking for salvation
as my hair tries to escape the scene.
While the men are at play
I answer: I haven't written
my character as a mother. I am
made a gift, so great
and lesser than this chair.
Quiet and still –
Alone with the breeze.

Acknowledgements

Mathilde Blind, 'Anne Hathaway's Cottage' and 'Anne Hathaway,' from *Birds of Passage: Songs of the Orient and Occident* (London: Chatto & Windus, 1895)

Wendy Cope, 'The Marriage', by permission from Faber and Faber

Charles Dibdin, 'A Love Dittie,' from *Hannah Hewit, Volume III* (London: C. Dibdin, 1796)

Carol Ann Duffy, 'Item I gyve unto my wief my second best bed…' from *New Selected Poems 1984-2004* (Picador, 2004). Originally published in *The World's Wife* (Macmillan, 1999). Reprinted by permission of the author.

John Harris, 'Shottery', from *Shakspere's Shrine* (London, Hamilton Adams, 1866)

William Ireland, 'Verses to Anne Hathaway,' from *Miscellaneous Papers and Legal Instruments* (London: Cooper and Graham, 1796)

Anna Catherine Markham, 'Anne Hathaway Alone at Avon' from *The Lyric Year: One Hundred Poems*, ed. Ferdinand Earle (NY: Mitchell Kennerley, 1912)

Constance Naden, 'In the Lanes Between Stratford and Shottery,' from *The Complete Poetical Works of Constance Naden* (London: Bickers and Son, 1894)

Roger Pringle, 'Making Of Her Will' from *Thanks to Shakespeare: Poems by Roger Pringle* (Halford: The Celandine Press, 2012)

John Agard FRSL is an Afro-Guyanese playwright, poet and children's writer, now living in Britain. In 2012, he was selected for the Queen's Gold Medal for Poetry.

Vasiliki Albedo is a Greek poet and renewable energy strategist. She is the winner of The Poetry Society's 2022 Stanza competition.

Andre Bagoo is a poet, writer, and essayist. He lives in Trinidad with his dog Chaplin.

Robert Bal is a London poet living and working as a therapist on stolen First Nations land in so-called Canada.

Liam Bates lives in Lancashire. His debut collection, *Human Townsperson*, is available from Broken Sleep Books.

Sally Bayley first learnt how to read and write by speaking and singing out the sounds of poetry.

Charlie Baylis' first collection of poetry is *A fondness for the colour green* (Broken Sleep Books). He spends his spare time completely adrift of reality.

Mathilde Blind (1841-1896) was a German-born poet who spent most of her career as an early feminist writer in England.

Jane Burn is autistic. She's a working-class, pansexual, polymathic off-grid enthusiast, essayist, and research junkie. She writes a lot.

Wendy Cope's most recent poetry collection is *Anecdotal Evidence*. Her collected poems will appear in 2024.

Hannah Copley is a poet, lecturer and editor. Her first collection, *Speculum* (Broken Sleep Books), was published in 2021.

Lesley Curwen is a broadcaster, poet and sailor living in Plymouth. She writes about storms, loss and rescue.

Rishi Dastidar's third collection, *Neptune's Projects*, is published in the UK by Nine Arches Press.

Olga Dermott-Bond has published two pamphlets. Her first full collection *Frieze* (Nine Arches Press) is out October 2023.

Imtiaz Dharker is a poet, artist and video film maker. She was awarded the Queen's Gold Medal for Poetry in 2014.

Charles Dibdin (1745-1814) was an author and composer best known for the music for David Garrick's Stratford Jubilee in 1769.

Carol Ann Duffy is Professor and Creative Director of The Writing School at Manchester Metropolitan University. In 2021 she received the International Golden Wreath Award for lifetime achievement in poetry.

Ella Duffy is the author of *Rootstalk* (Hazel Press) and *New Hunger* (Smith|Doorstop). Her work has appeared in *The Poetry Review, The London Magazine* and *The Rialto*, among others.

Taylor Edmonds is a poet from South Wales. Her debut poetry pamphlet *Back Teeth* is published with Broken Sleep Books.

Barbara Everett taught English at Hull, Cambridge and Oxford, writes criticism and poems, and has a daughter and two grandchildren.

Ewan Fernie is Professor at the Shakespeare Institute and Culture Lead for the College of Arts and Law, University of Birmingham.

Tommy Oliver Sam Flynn: 'I enjoy playing football. When I am older I am going to be a footballer or darts player.'

Paul Francis lives in Much Wenlock, and is active in the West Midlands poetry scene. His website is www.paulfranciswrites.co.uk

Wendy Freeman is a Poet and Artist living in Stratford-upon-Avon.

Jo Gatford is a Shakespeare Institute alumna and the author of *The Woman's Part*, a collection inspired by Shakespeare's women.

Kathy Gee worked in heritage. Author of three poetry collections, she is a trustee of the Shakespeare Birthplace Trust. https://www.brainginger.co.uk

Dr. Neal Hall is an internationally award-winning poet, who has composed poetry and performed readings throughout the U.S. and internationally.

Susanna Shakespeare Hall (1583-1649) was the eldest daughter of Anne and William Shakespeare.

John Harris (1820-1884) was a Cornish tin-miner, prolific poet, and fellow of the Royal Society.

Justina Hart is a poet, novelist and non-fiction writer based in the Midlands, whose ancestors hail from Shottery. justinahart.com

Lucy Holme is a writer living in Cork, Ireland. Her pamphlet, *Temporary Stasis*, is out now from Broken Sleep Books.

Maisie Ireland: 'I like playing games. When I'm older I would like to be a vet. I enjoy playing with my dog.'

William Ireland (1775-1835), the son of engraver Samuel Ireland, was a writer best remembered for his Shakespeare forgeries.

Luke Kennard's collection *Notes on the Sonnets* won the 2021 Forward Prize. He lectures at the University of Birmingham.

Fiona Larkin's pamphlets are *Vital Capacity* (Broken Sleep, 2022) and *A Dovetail of Breath* (Rack Press, 2020). Her debut collection *Rope of Sand* is forthcoming in 2023 with Pindrop Press.

Nina Lewis was Worcestershire Poet Laureate 2017-18. Her pamphlets *Fragile Houses* and *Patience* are published by V. Press. ninalewispoet.wordpress.com

Len Lukowski is a queer writer based in Glasgow. His first pamphlet was published by Broken Sleep Books in 2022.

Anna Catherine Markham (1859-1938) was an American poet, teacher, and secretary of the Poetry Society of America.

Louise Mather is a writer from Northern England and founding editor of *Acropolis Journal*. Twitter: @lm2020uk IG: louise.mather.uk

Andrea Mbarushimana is a Coventry-based writer and workshop leader. Her latest pamphlet 'Fatbergs' is available from KFS Press.

Fokkina McDonnell holds a Northern Writers' Award and has three collections and a pamphlet. Fokkina now lives in The Netherlands.

Jennifer McLean is a writer and English teacher from Yorkshire, now living near Stratford-upon-Avon.

Andrew McMillan lives in Manchester.

Stuart McPherson is a poet from Leicestershire. He has published the collections *Obligate Carnivore* and *End Ceremonies* via Broken Sleep Books.

Jessica Mehta, Ph.D., is a multi-award-winning interdisciplinary artist and poet. As an Aniyunwiya (citizen of the Cherokee Nation), space, place, and history are the driving forces in much of her work. Learn more at www.thischerokeerose.com

Jenny Mitchell won the Poetry Book Awards with a collection that's on a university syllabus. Her third book, *Resurrection of a Black Man*, is published by Indigo Dreams.

Constance Naden (1858-1889) was a Birmingham poet and philosopher who published two volumes of poetry often focussed on the natural world, ethics, and morality.

Grace Nichols is a Guyanese/British poet who has written many books for both adults and children. She was awarded the Queen's Gold Medal for Poetry in 2021.

Richard O'Brien is a Lecturer in Creative Writing at Northumbria University. He completed his practice-based PhD at the Shakespeare Institute in 2017.

Yewande Okuleye is a poet, artist, and medical historian. Her poetry examines birth, life, death, and everything in between.

Emilia Olivia: 'I am nine years old and my hobbies are gymnastics and singing.'

Caleb Parkin, Bristol City Poet 2020-22, is published widely in journals, commissions; *This Fruiting Body*; three pamphlets | www.calebparkin.com

Roger Pringle is Former Director of Shakespeare Birthplace Trust and Stratford Poetry Festival. He's written on Shakespeare and Stratford-upon-Avon and published poetry collections.

Emma Purshouse is a novelist and performance poet. She was third prize winner of the 2021 National Poetry Competition. www.emmapurshouse.co.uk

Yousif M. Qasmiyeh is the author of *Writing the Camp* (shortlisted for the RSL Ondaatje Prize and a PBS recommendation) and *Eating the Archive*, both published by Broken Sleep Books.

Sam Quill is a poet, musician and songwriter who lives and works in London.

Judith Shakespeare Quiney (1585-1662) was the youngest daughter of Anne and William Shakespeare.

Dean Rhetoric is a poet living in Manchester. His debut collection, *Foundry Songs*, is out now via Broken Sleep Books.

Rochelle Roberts is a writer and editor. Her debut pamphlet *Your Retreating Shadow* was published by Broken Sleep Books in 2022.

Amber Rollinson is a writer from Bristol. Her debut poetry pamphlet was published by Broken Sleep Books in June 2022.

Rachel Sambrooks is a writer/performer based in Birmingham, her debut pamphlet 'Harpy' (Palewell Press) was published in 2020. www.rachelsambrooks.com

George Sandifer-Smith has published two books of poetry and one children's book. He lives with his wife and their cat.

Hal Algernon Sandle-Keynes: 'I love music and writing. I play the guitar and am a skilled tennis player.'

Anna Saunders is the Founding Director of Cheltenham Poetry Festival and the author of seven collections of poetry, her latest being *The Prohibition of Touch* (Indigo Dreams, 2022).

William Shakespeare (1564-1616) was a poet and playwright, and husband of Anne Shakespeare.

Genevieve Anne Marragold Stead: 'I am nine and a half years old and I love to dance. I have a brother called Leif.'

Julie Stevens writes poems that cover many themes, but often engages with the problems of disability.

Taylor Strickland is a poet and translator from the US. He is the author of *Commonplace Book* and *Dastrasm/Delirium*.

Elizabeth Sylvia lives in the New England. She explores complicated feelings about Shakespeare's women in her book *None But Witches*.

Athens-born **Kostya Tsolakis** edits *harana poetry*. *Greekling*, his debut collection, will be published by Nine Arches Press in October 2023.

Carina Vallera-Satchwell: 'I love spending time with my family. I also love ballet and all kinds of animals.'

U. G. Világos is an internationally acclaimed poet, well known for his collection *The Lark Sings Wind*, winner of the Continental Poesis medal.

Cat Weatherill is a performance storyteller, performing internationally at storytelling and literature festivals, on national radio and television and at schools throughout the country.

Rowan Williams is the author of several collections of poetry as well as numerous studies in theology, and currently lives in Wales.

Ayşegül Yıldırım's debut pamphlet, *Plants Beyond Desire*, was published in 2022.

LAY OUT YOUR ANNE-REST